GO HANG A SALAMI! I'M A LASAGNA HOG!

Palindrome (păl´ĭn-drōm´), *n. a word, verse or sentence which reads the same backward and forward (e.g., Go hang a salami! I'm a lasagna hog!).*

GO HANG A SALAMI!

I'M A LASAGNA HOG!

and Other Palindromes

by JON AGEE

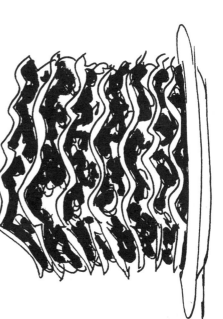

A Sunburst Book

Farrar · Straus · Giroux

To Hannah

Library of Congress catalog card number: 91-31319
Published in Canada by HarperCollins*Canada*Ltd
Printed and bound in the United States of America
First edition, 1991. Sunburst edition, 1994

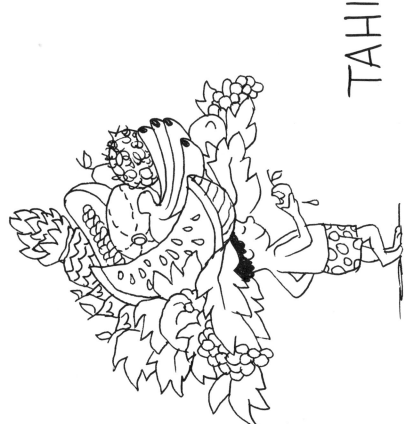

TAHITI HAT

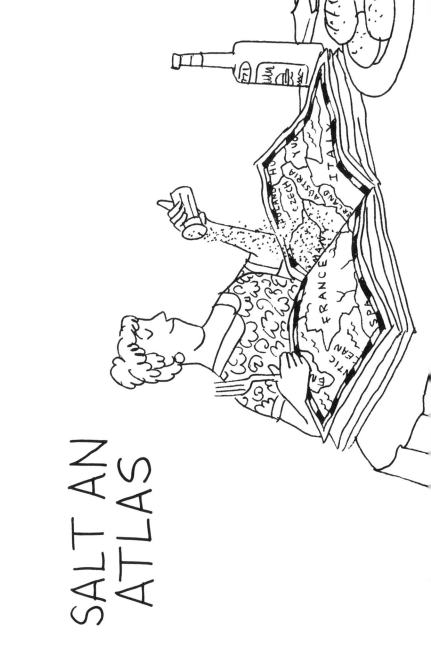

SALT AN
ATLAS

SMART RAMS

STAR RATS

NEIL, AN ALIEN

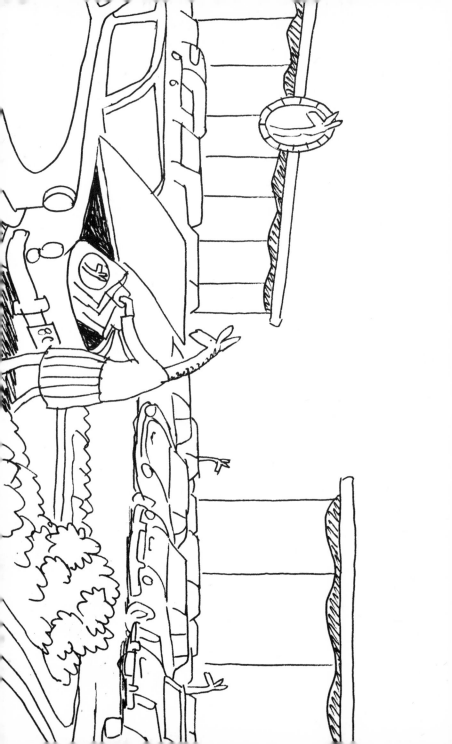

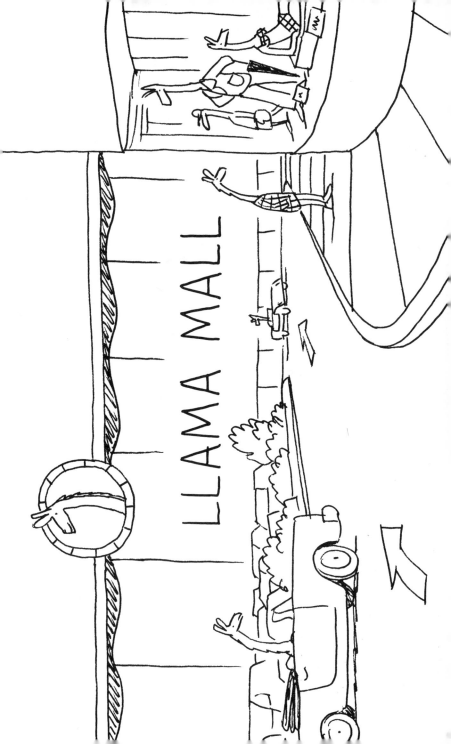

LAST EGG GETS AL

A CAR, A MAN, A MARACA

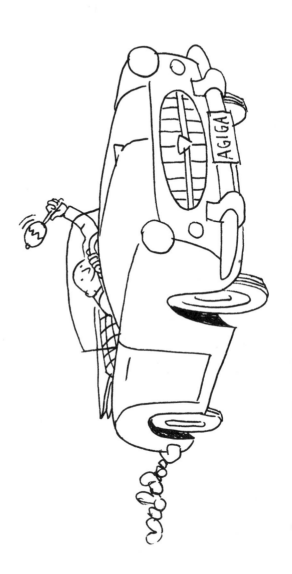

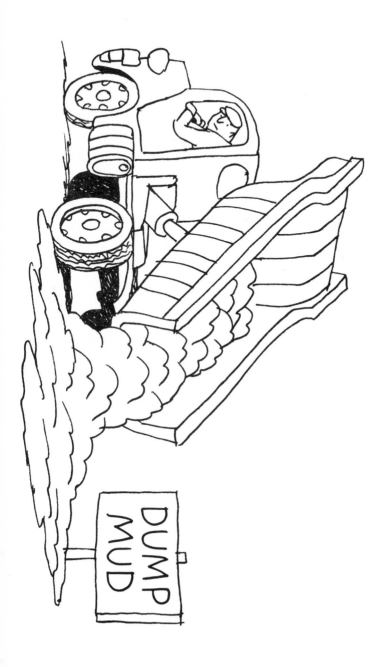

EMIL'S NIECE, IN SLIME

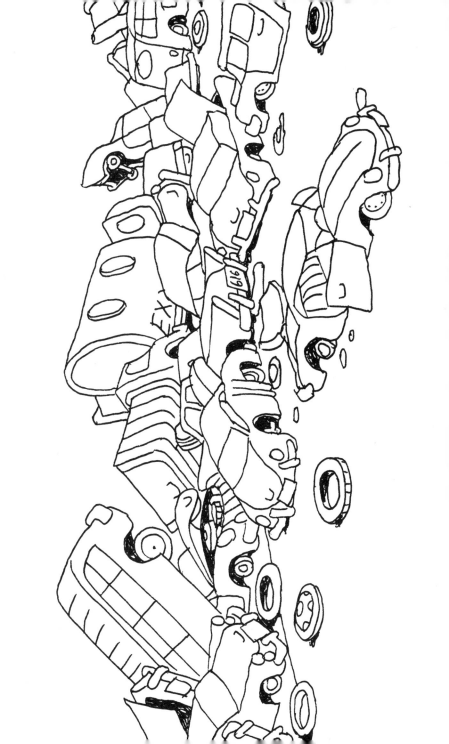

ED IS ON NO SIDE

SUB'S KNOB BONKS BUS

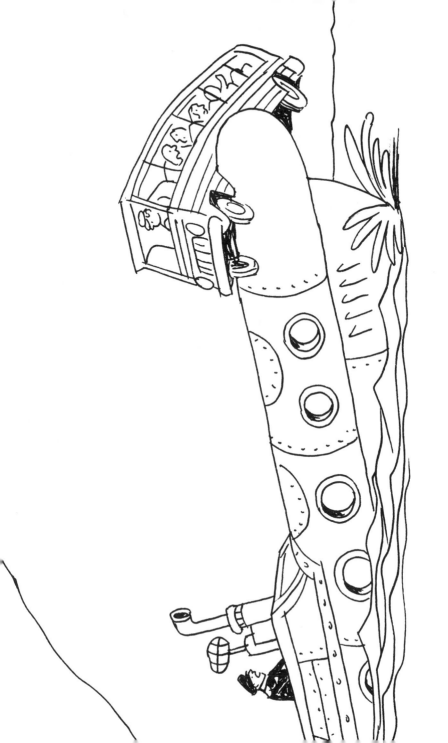

EMILY'S SASSY LIME

DROWSY SWORD

TABOO BAT

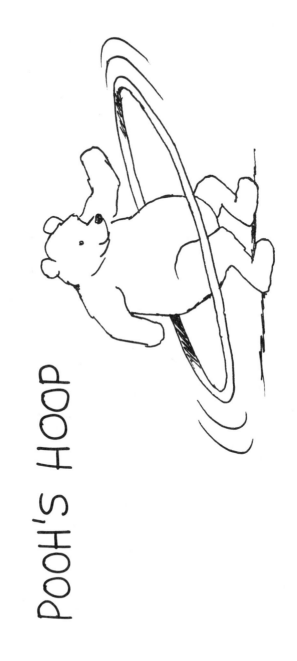

POOH'S HOOP

DAMON, A NOMAD

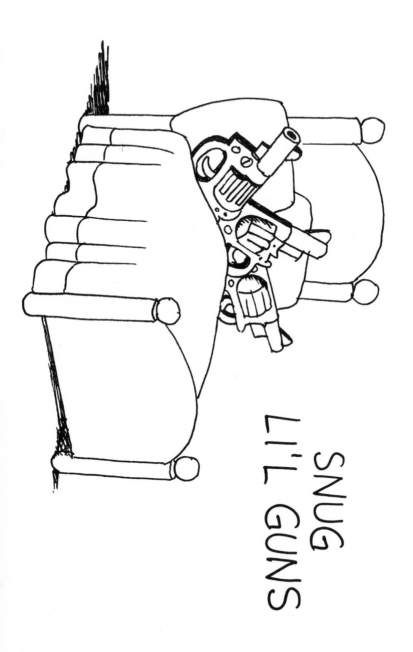

SNUG
LI'L GUNS

ELSIE'S ON A NOSE ISLE

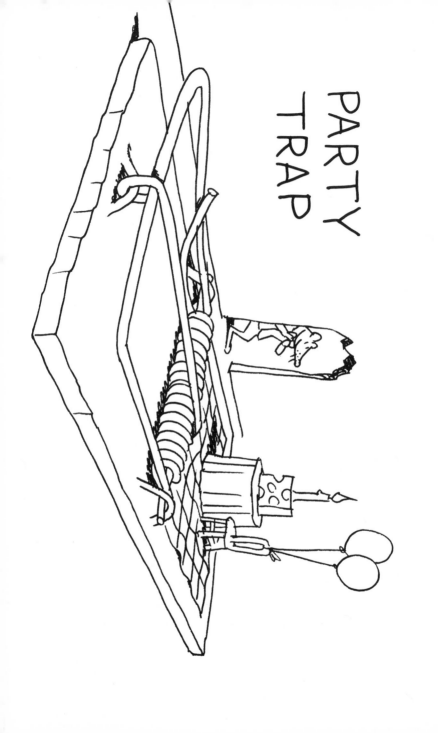

PARTY
TRAP

OOZY RAT
IN A SANITARY ZOO

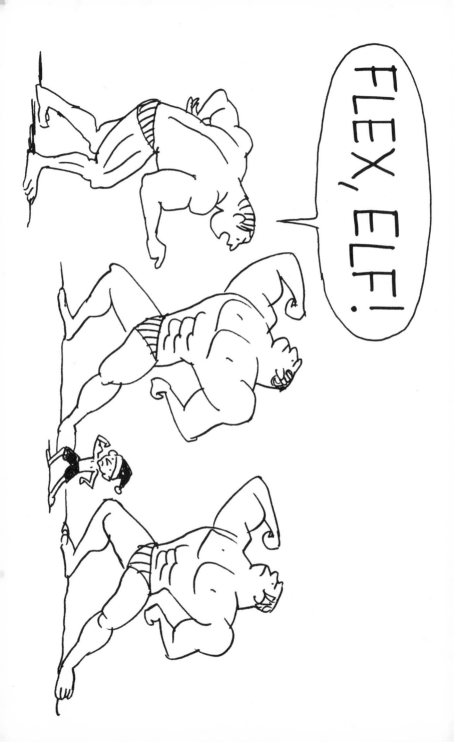

Thanks to

Dan Allen, Tom Bassmann, John Baumann,
Russell Busch, Dan Feigelson, Holly McGhee,
Phil Warton, Maria Warton-Bennett and
Stephen Wolf for their contributions.

The figure of Pooh is based on the original illustrations
by E. H. Shepard by permission of the Trustees of the Pooh
Properties, the Executor of E. H. Shepard, and the E. H.
Shepard Trust.

Agee (ā´-jē), *n. 1: Jon, b. 1960– U.S. author and illustrator whose books include* Ludlow Laughs, The Incredible Painting of Felix Clousseau *(an* ALA Notable Book*), and* The Return of Freddy LeGrand *(a* School Library Journal Best Book*). 2: an extinct flightless bird.*